Fast & Funny
JOKES & RIDDLES

By Martha Smith

Watermill Press

Cover design and illustration by Rod L. Gonzalez

Printed in the United States of America.

10 9 8 7 6 5 4 3 2 1

COWBOY: "What kind of saddle do you want? One with a horn, or one without?"

DUDE: "Without, I guess. You don't seem to have much traffic around here."

What do you get when you cross an elephant with a jaguar?

A sportscar with a big trunk.

What increases its value by one-half when turned upside-down?

The number six.

Which part of a fish weighs the most?

The scales.

What does a geologist have in common with a guitar player?

They both like rock.

Why can't a man living in New York City be buried west of the Mississippi River?

Because he's still alive.

What is it that no man wishes to have, yet no man wishes to lose?

A bald head.

What three-letter word becomes fewer when two letters are added to it?

Few.

TEACHER: "Why didn't you answer me?"

PUPIL: "I did — I shook my head."

TEACHER: "Oh, I see. You expected me to hear it rattle!"

Why does a stork stand on one leg?

Because if he took two legs off the ground he would fall down.

WILLIE: "Why are you running that steam roller over your field?"

SILLY: "I thought it would be fun to raise *mashed* potatoes this year!"

What can I see that you cannot, that is nearer to you than to me?

The back of your head.

How can you go without sleep for seven nights and still not be tired?

Sleep during the day.

Why did the elephant leave the circus?

Because he was tired of working for peanuts.

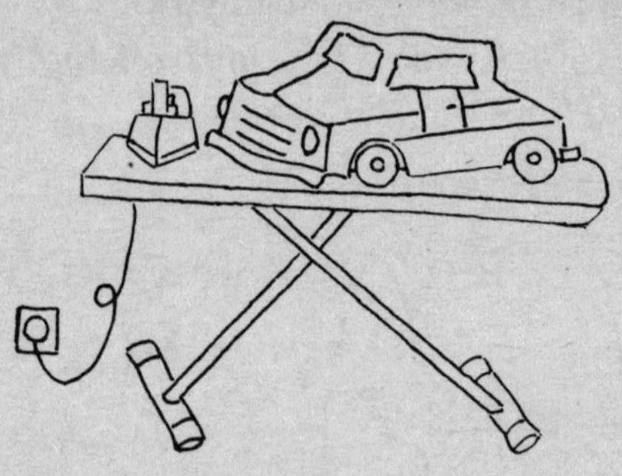

Car wash attendant, looking at the battered car: "Sorry. We *wash* cars—we don't *iron* them!"

What did the mayonnaise say to the refrigerator?

"Close the door, I'm dressing!"

TEACHER: "Your essay, 'My Dog,' is exactly the same as your brother's."

BILLY: "It's the same dog."

What is more useful when it is broken?

An egg.

What would a cannibal be who ate his mother's sister?

An aunt-eater.

Why are weary people like automobile wheels?

Because they are tired.

What is the best way to carry water in a sieve?

Freeze it first.

TEACHER: "Bobbie, why is your composition on milk only one page long, when the assignment called for *two* pages?"

BOBBIE: "I wrote about *condensed* milk!"

MARTIAN BOY: "Mom, please make me a sandwich."

MARTIAN MOTHER: (impatiently) "You'll just have to wait a minute! I've only got *four* hands!"

What time is it when the clock strikes 13?

Time to get the clock fixed.

What is worse than a giraffe with a sore throat?

A centipede with corns.

PETE: "Did you know the bakery is making bread out of yeast and shoe polish?"

MIKE: "Why?"

PETE: "It's for people who want to rise and shine!"

Why is a puppy like a brand new penny?

Each has a head and a tail.

TEACHER: "Yes, Mary. What is it?"

MARY: "I don't want to scare you, teacher, but my daddy said if I didn't bring home better grades, *some*one is due for a spanking!"

What is the best butter in the world?

A goat.

What did one flea say to the other?

"Shall we walk, or take a dog?"

LIONESS: "Son, what are you doing?"

CUB: "I'm chasing a hunter around a tree."

LIONESS: "How many times have I told you not to play with your food!"

What do we often see made, but never see *after* it is made?

A noise.

DANNY: "Mom, would you spank me for something I didn't do?"

MOM: "Of course not, dear. Why do you ask?"

DANNY: "Well, I didn't do my homework."

What did the boy octopus say to the girl octopus?

"I want to hold your hand, hand, hand, hand, hand......"

What did the winner lose in the race?

Her breath.

When is a door not a door?

When it is ajar.

What is over your head but under your hat?

Your hair.

If you drop a white hat into the Red Sea, what will it become?

Wet.

What gets lost when you stand up?

Your lap.

What is the difference between the North Pole and the South Pole?

All the difference in the world.

WILLY:
"Do you know how deep that river is?"

SILLY:
"It must be shallow, 'cause it only goes up to that little duck's stomach!"

SALLY: "I've added these figures twelve times, teacher."

TEACHER: "Good work, Sally."

SALLY: "And here are my twelve answers!"

MOTORIST:
"I'm sorry to tell you I've killed your cat. But I've come to replace him."

LITTLE OLD LADY:
"How good are you at catching mice?"

How do sailors get their clothes clean?

They throw them overboard, and they're washed ashore.

How can you divide four apples among five people, equally?

Make applesauce.

JACK: "Did I ever tell you about the time I came face to face with a lion?"

JILL: "No. What happened?"

JACK: "There I was, without a gun. The lion roared and crept closer and closer and closer..."

JILL: "What did you do?"

JACK: "I moved on to the next cage!"

What is higher without the head, than *with* the head?

A pillow.

Why does a fireman wear red suspenders?

To keep his pants up.

What is it which *will be* yesterday, and *was* tomorrow?

Today.

A lawyer sat in the dentist's chair, seemingly lost in thought. When the dentist was finally ready for him, the lawyer said, "Do you swear to pull the tooth and nothing but the tooth?"

What gets bigger when you take more away from it?

A hole.

What is worse than finding a worm in an apple?

Finding half a worm.

What word do you always pronounce wrong?

Wrong.

PAM:
"Did you change the water in the goldfish bowl?"

SAM:
"No, they haven't drunk it all yet."

To what man do men always take their hats off?

The barber.

FARMER:
"How did you come to fall in the pond?"

BILLY:
"I didn't come to fall in. I came to fish."

What nut is like a sneeze?

A cashew.

What comes right up to the door but never comes into the house?

The sidewalk.

How many books can you put into an empty school bag?

One. After that, the bag isn't empty.

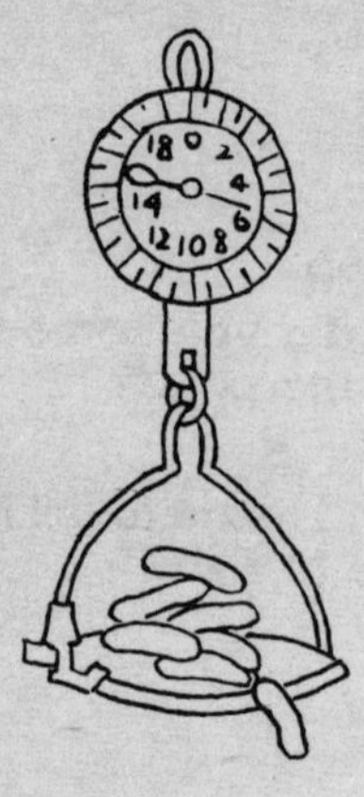

Mr. Green is a butcher. He is six feet tall and wears a size 10 shoe and a size 40 suit. What does he weigh?

Meat.

What is taller sitting than standing?

A dog.

CUSTOMER: "Do you sell dog meat?"

BUTCHER: "Only if they come in on a leash and have some money."

What sings and has eight legs?

A quartet.

BILLY: "More cake, please."

MOTHER: "If you eat any more cake you'll burst!"

BILLY: "Then pass the cake and get out of the way!"

What is full of holes and yet can hold water?

A sponge.

Three hard-of-hearing people met on the street one day.

"Windy, isn't it?" said one.

"No, it's Thursday," said the second.

"So am I," said the third. "Let's all have a soda."

What makes more noise than a pig caught under a fence?

Two pigs.

Born at the same time as the world, destined to live as long as the world, yet never five weeks old. What is it?

The moon.

What does a ghost call his mother and father?

Transparents.

Why is a watchdog bigger by night than he is by day?

Because he is let out at night and taken in in the morning.

STUDENT: "I don't think I deserve a zero on this paper!"

TEACHER: "I don't either, but it's the lowest mark I can give."

When you lose something, why do you always find it in the last place you look?

Because you stop looking when you find it.

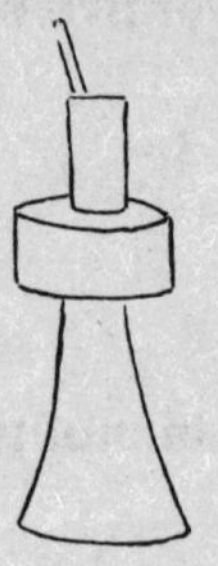

LITTLE BOY: "Make me a malted."

SODA JERK (waving his hand): "Poof! You're a malted!"

What has eighteen legs and catches flies?

A baseball team.

What goes up and down, but stays in one place?

A road.

Why do they say a rooster is a very particular bird?

Because he won't lend anyone his comb.

Those with eyes don't have any heads, and those with heads don't have any eyes. What are they?

Pins and needles.

MOTHER: "Son, I heard you played baseball today, instead of going to school."

SON: "That's a lie, Mother, and I have a string of fish to prove it."

Why was the little strawberry worried?

Because his mother and father were in a jam.

What contains more feet in winter than in summer?

An outdoor ice-skating rink.

What does a tooth have that a tree has?

Roots.

What can speak every language, though it never went to school?

An echo.

Why do dragons sleep in the daytime?

Because they like to hunt (k)nights.

What is it which has never been felt, seen or heard, never existed, and still has a name?

Nothing.

TEACHER:
"What is a comet?"

PUPIL:
"A star with a tail."

TEACHER:
"Name one."

PUPIL:
"Lassie."

Two people were standing on a bridge. One was the father of the other's son. What relation were the two people?

Husband and wife.

On which side does a chicken have the most feathers?

The outside.

Why does a rabbit have a shiny nose?

Because its powder puff is at the other end.

What is the difference between a hungry man and a glutton?

One eats to live. The other lives to eat.

DENTIST:
"What kind of filling do you want in your tooth?"

JEANNIE:
"Chocolate."

What do you hold without touching it?

Your breath.

Who is not my sister or brother, but still the child of my father?

Me.

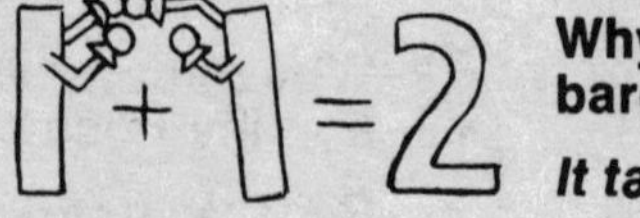

Why is a quarrel like a bargain?

It takes two to make it.

What is it that has four legs and only one foot?

A bed.

What's the hardest thing about learning to roller-skate?

The pavement.

What kind of serpents are like babies' toys?

Rattlers.

Why was the mother flea crying?

Because her children had gone to the dogs.

What can't be seen, but is everywhere?

The air.

TEACHER: "If you add 2,367 and 535, multiply by 6 and divide by 5, what will you get?"

STUDENT: "The wrong answer."

What state doesn't feel so good? *Ill.*

What state is a doctor? *Md.*

What state is a father? *Pa.*

What state is a number? *Tenn.*

What runs around the whole yard, yet never moves?

The fence.

SILLY: "Is it true that tigers won't hurt you if you run away from them?"

MILLY: "Depends how fast you run!"

What key is the hardest to turn?

A donkey.

What goes ninety-nine, thump, ninety-nine, thump?

A centipede with a wooden leg.

Why are pianos like good people?

Because they're upright and grand.

What do bees do with their honey?

They cell it.

What walks on one foot and hums like a bee?

A top.

What is smaller than an ant's mouth?

What goes into it.

What has teeth and never eats?

A comb.

What did one hippopotamus say to another hippopotamus?

Nothing. Hippopotamuses can't talk.

What's the difference between a mother and a barber?

The barber has razors to shave. The mother has shavers to raise.

What is it that we have in December that we don't have in any other month?

The letter D.

MOTHER: "How did you do on your first day at school?"

SON: "Not so good, I guess. I have to go back tomorrow."

When was beef the highest it has ever been?

When the cow jumped over the moon.

What do ghosts eat for breakfast?

Ghost Toasties, and evaporated milk.

How does a witch tell time?

With a witch watch.

When do 2 and 2 make more than 4?

When they make 22.

Why is a snake a careless animal?

Because he loses his skin.

Three girls are under one umbrella, but none of them gets wet. How can this be?

It isn't raining.

What is the difference between here and there?

The letter T.

If you put three ducks into a crate, what would you have?

A box of quackers.

What is it that everyone wishes for, but wants to get rid of as soon as they have it?

A good appetite.

What animal took the most luggage into the Ark, and what animal took the least?

The elephant took his trunk; the rooster only a comb.

What has neither flesh, bone, nor nails—yet has four fingers and a thumb?

A glove.

Why is a healthy boy like the United States?

Because he has a good constitution.

If twelve make a dozen, how many make a million?

Very few.

Why is a locomotive like a stick of gum?

One goes choo choo, the other goes chew chew.

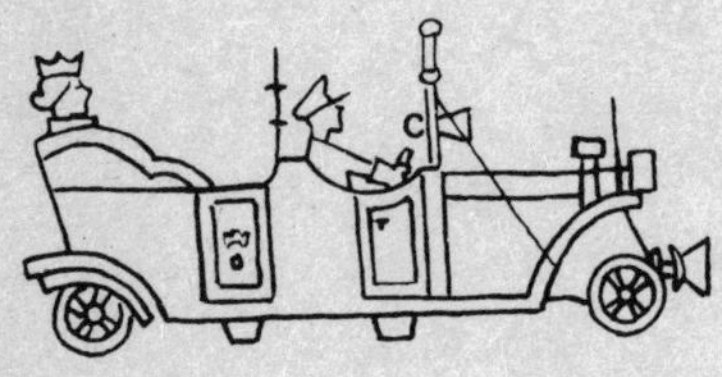

Who dares to sit before the Queen of England with his hat on?

Her chauffeur.

What keeps the moon in place?

Its beams.

TEACHER: "Use the word *geometry* in a sentence."

STUDENT: "The little acorn grew and grew, and one day it woke up and said, 'Gee ahm-a-tree!' "

What is the difference between a prizefighter and a man with a cold?

One knows his blows, the other blows his nose.

How can you change a pumpkin into another vegetable?

Throw it up into the air and it will come down squash.

What is a professor?

A textbook wired for sound.

What is a volcano?

A mountain with hiccups.

What gallops everywhere on its head?

A horseshoe nail.

What room has no walls, no doors, no floors, and no windows?

A mushroom.

What is it that is always behind in time?

The back of a clock.

Why is the game of baseball like a buckwheat cake?

Both depend on the batter.

What did the big hand on the clock say to the little hand?

"I'll be around in an hour."

What is it that is black and white and red all over?

A bashful zebra.

What breaks but does not fall? What falls but does not break?

Day breaks and night falls.

ROSIE: "Did you know that it takes three sheep to make a sweater?"

POSIE: "Gee — I didn't even know they could knit!"

What is the best paper to make a kite out of?

Fly paper.

What is the biggest jewel in all the world?

A baseball diamond.

BABY CORN: **"Mommy, who brought me?"**

MOTHER CORN: **"Hush, child. The stalk brought you."**

DENNIS: **"Mom, I just knocked over the ladder in the back yard."**

MOTHER: **"You'd better tell your father."**

DENNIS: **"He knows. He was on it."**

What bird is sad?

A blue-bird.

What kind of a man is a dentist?

One with a lot of pull.

Why did the man take sugar and cream to the movies?

He heard there was a new serial.

When is a boat affectionate?

When it hugs the shore.

What is it that has a face but no head, hands but no feet, travels everywhere and is usually running?

A watch.

GIRL: **"Mom, may I have ten cents for a man who's crying outside."**

MOTHER: **"What is he crying about?"**

GIRL: **"Ice cream—only ten cents!"**

What did the hen say when she saw a plate of scrambled eggs?

What a bunch of mixed-up kids!

Why are fishermen so stingy?

Because their business makes them sell-fish.

What has four wheels and flies?

A garbage truck.

What question can never be answered "yes"?

"Are you asleep?"

What travels without feet and speaks without a mouth?

A letter.

What bird would be supposed to lift the heaviest weight?

A crane.

Tell me two things you can never eat for breakfast.

Lunch and dinner.

If you lived in a cemetery, with what would you open the gate?

A skeleton key.

What belongs to you but is used more often by others?

Your name.

Why are fish smarter than birds?

Because they live in schools.

What goes through a door, but never goes in or comes out?

The keyhole.

What has 88 keys but can't unlock a single door?

A piano.

What is a bull when he's sleeping?

A bull-dozer.

What two letters of the alphabet contain nothing?

M. T.

What is it that has four legs, eats oats, has a tail, and sees equally well from both ends?

A blind mule.

What state is round at both ends and high in the middle?

Ohio.

Why do little pigs eat so much?

To make hogs of themselves.

BILL: "Dad, is it true that the law of gravity keeps us on this planet?"

DAD: "Yes, son."

BILL: "What did we do before the law was passed?"

What has a bed but never sleeps?

A river.

What is horse sense?

Just stable thinking.

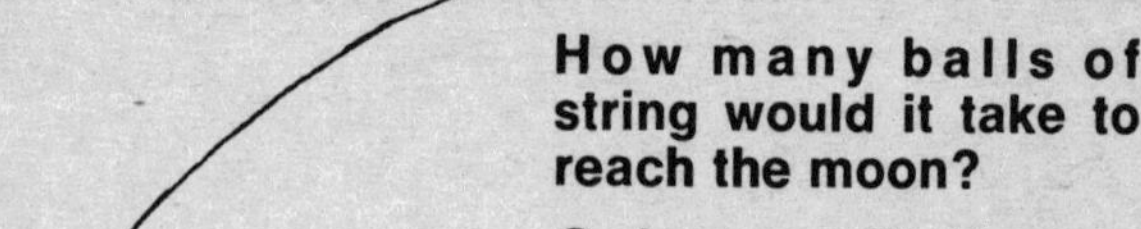

How many balls of string would it take to reach the moon?

Only one — if it were long enough.

What bird is very rude?

A mockingbird.

Why was the giant Goliath astonished when David hit him with a stone?

Because such a thing had never before entered his head.

What can go through water and not get wet?

Sunlight.

What can you hold in your left hand that you can't hold in your right hand?

Your right elbow.

What table hasn't a leg to stand on?

The multiplication table.

Why does a giraffe eat very little?

Because he must make a little go a long way.

What doesn't ask questions but must be answered?

The telephone.

What are two flowers that should decorate the zoo?

A dandelion and a tiger lily.

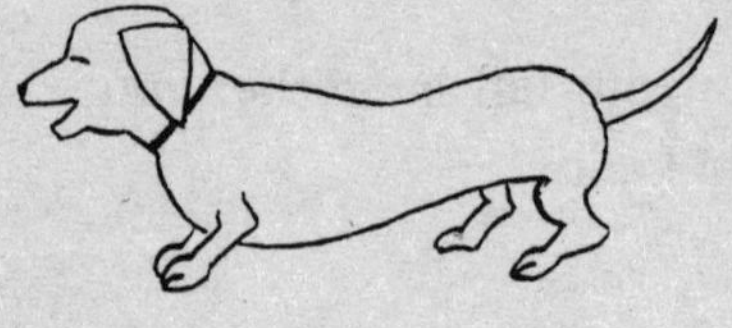

Why is a dog's tail like the heart of a tree?

Because it's farthest from the bark.

WILLIE: "I've been seeing spots before my eyes."

MILLIE: "Did you see a doctor?"

WILLIE: "No, just spots."

What is the best way to swallow a door?

Bolt it.

What has two tongues but no mouth?

A pair of sneakers.

If eight eggs cost twenty-six cents, how many eggs can you buy for a cent and a quarter?

Eight eggs.

What bites but isn't alive?

Frost.

Why would a barber rather shave ten men from Boston than one man from San Francisco?

Because he would get ten times as much money.

I occur once in every minute, twice in every moment, and yet not once in a billion years. What am I?

***The letter* M.**

When is a piece of wood like a Queen?

When it is a ruler.

What flower does a person carry around all year?

Tulips.

When is a piece of string like a stick of wood?

When it has knots in it.

FIRST BOY: "Why are you always snapping your fingers?"

SECOND BOY: "To keep the lions away."

FIRST BOY: "There isn't a lion within a hundred miles of here!"

SECOND BOY: "Sure works, doesn't it?"

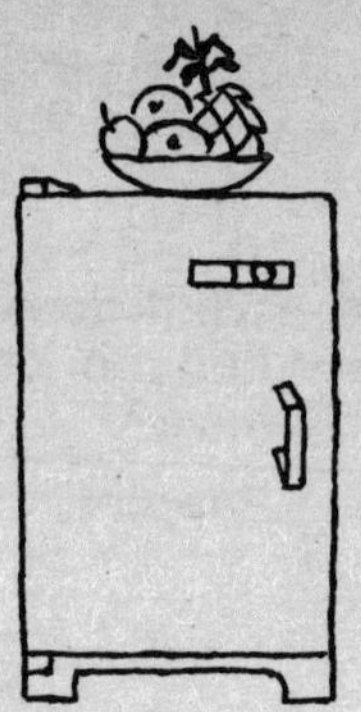

What is it that stays hot even if you put it in a refrigerator?

Pepper.

What is everybody doing at the same time?

Growing older.

What's green and has wheels?

Grass. I was just kidding about the wheels.

The greater it is the less can be seen. What is it?

Darkness.

REPORTER: "What made you risk your life to save your friend?"

BOY HERO: "I *had* to do it—he was wearing my skates!"

What does a dog have that no other animals have?

Puppies.

What is the best way to make a coat last?

Make the pants first.

What has four legs, a pouch and a trunk?

A kangaroo going on a trip.

What did Paul Revere say at the end of his ride?

Whoa!

How can you tell that the train is gone?

When you see its tracks.

What is the quietest game played?

Bowling — you can hear a pin drop.

Which travels faster, heat or cold?

Heat. You can catch cold.

What gives milk and has one horn?

A milk truck.

Why did Tommie take a ruler to bed with him?

To see how long he slept.

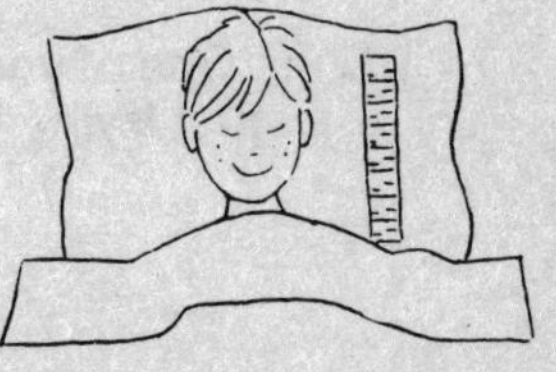

What is a pickle?

A cucumber in a sour mood.

FARMER: **"What are you doing up in that tree, young man?"**

BOY: **"One of your apples fell down, sir, and I was just trying to put it back."**

What fish may be said to be out of place?

A perch in a bird cage.

What falls often, but never gets hurt?

Rain.

Why is your hand like a hardware store?

It has nails.

Who always goes to bed with his shoes on?

A horse.

What roof never keeps out the wet?

The roof of your mouth.

What animal has the smallest appetite?

A moth. It just eats holes.

DINER: "Do you serve crabs here?"
WAITER: "We serve anyone, sir."

TEACHER: "Do you think carrots are healthy?"
STUDENT: "Well, I've never heard one complain."

What can you swallow that can also swallow you?
Water.

What did one ghost say to the other?
"Do you believe in people?"

What is it you cannot see, but is always before you?
The future.

When does a man have four hands?

When he doubles his fists.

At what time of day was Adam created?

A little before Eve.

HOSTESS:
"They tell me you love music."

GUEST:
"Yes, but never mind — keep right on playing."

What is bought by the yard and worn by the foot?

A carpet.

What can pass before the sun without making a shadow?

The wind.

What is the best way to catch a fish?

Have someone throw it to you.

SILLY: "Do you believe in free speech?"

MILLY: "Of course I do."

SILLY: "Then may I make a long distance call on your telephone?"

What has two tails, six feet and four trunks?

An elephant with spare parts!

What did the adding machine say to the clerk?

"You can count on me!"

What fruit can you buy from an electric plant?

Currents.

What has four legs and flies?

Two birds.

The little daughter of a tire salesman saw triplets for the first time in a newspaper story. "Oh Mommy!" she exclaimed. "What do you think it says here?"

"I don't know, dear. What does it say?"

"It tells about a lady that had twins — and a *spare!*"

Why did the chicken cross the road?

For fowl reasons.

Why did the rabbit cross the road?

It was stapled to the chicken.

JIM: "London is the foggiest city in the world."

KIM: "No it's not. I've been to someplace even foggier."

JIM: "Where?"

KIM: "I have no idea. It was too foggy to tell!"

What kind of a table has no legs?

A timetable.

What's a raisin?

A worried grape.

Which is the strongest day of the week?

Sunday — all the rest are week (weak) days.

What goes under the water and over the water, yet never touches the water?

A woman crossing a bridge with a bucket of water on her head.

The teacher had been reading to the class about the rhinoceros family. When she finished reading she said, "Now, class, name some things that are very dangerous to get near to, and that have horns."

"Automobiles," Billy promptly answered.

A word has five letters. Take two away and leave only one. What is it?

St-one.

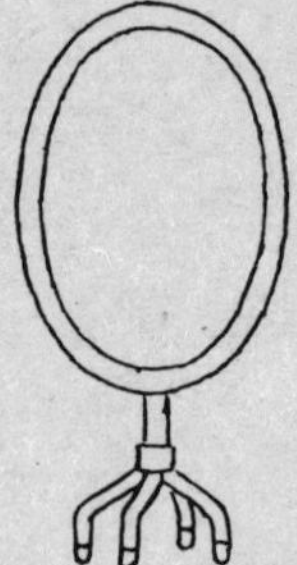

Look in my face and
I'm everybody;
Scratch my back and
I'm nobody.
Who am I?

A mirror.

What can let you see through walls?

Windows.

What runs but has no legs; has a mouth but cannot swallow?

A river.

Upon a hill there is a mill,
Around the mill there is a walk,
Under the walk there is a key.
Tell me the name of this mill.

Milwaukee.

What has a big head, but cannot think?

A cabbage.

What has ears but cannot hear?

A cornstalk.

SALLY: "We've got a new baby at our house."

SILLY: "Where did you get it?"

SALLY: "From Doctor Brown."

SILLY: "That's funny. We got *our* baby from him, too."

What lives in winter, dies in summer, and grows with its roots sticking upward?

An icicle.

Why does a dog turn around several times before lying down?

Because one good turn deserves another.

What animal has two humps and is found in Alaska?

A lost camel.

What is the difference between a beached ship and an airplane?

One grounds on the land, the other lands on the ground.

MIKE: "A steam roller ran over my uncle."

PETE: "What did you do?"

MIKE: "I just took him home and slipped him under the door."

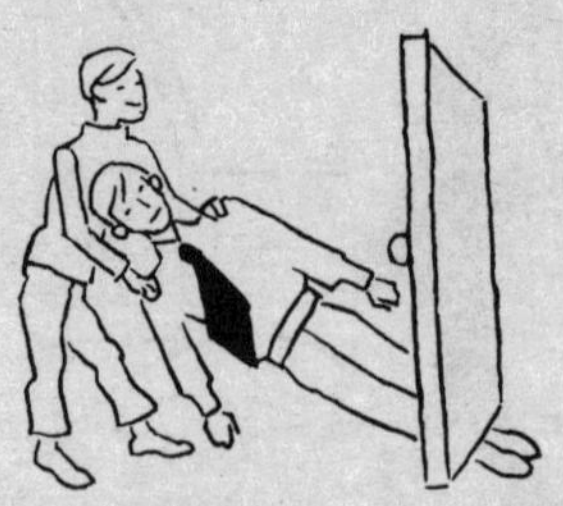

PAPA KANGAROO: "Margaret, where's the baby?"

MAMA KANGAROO: "My goodness! My pocket's been picked!"

In marble walls as white as milk,
Lined with a skin as soft as silk,
Within a fountain crystal clear,
A golden apple doth appear.
No gates there are to this stronghold,
Yet thieves break in and steal the gold.
What is it?

An egg.

What goes up every time the rain comes down?

Umbrellas.

What land do very small children like best?

Lapland.

What does everybody give and few take?

Advice.

DOCTOR: "What do you dream about at night?"

DOPEY: "Baseball."

DOCTOR: "Don't you ever dream about anything else?"

DOPEY: "No, just baseball, night after night."

DOCTOR: "You never dream about food?"

DOPEY: "What? And miss my turn at bat?"

What goes "zzub, zzub"?

A bee flying backwards.

What most resembles half a cheese?

The other half.

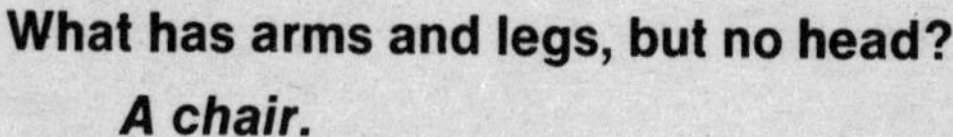

What has arms and legs, but no head?

A chair.

Why is a ship the most polite thing in the world?

Because it always proceeds with a bow.

FIRST GIRL: "We just got a new bike for my baby brother."

SECOND GIRL: "That sounds like a good trade to me."

What goes up but never comes down?

Your age.

What is filled every morning and emptied every night?

A shoe.

CHILD: "I'd like to buy a pillowcase."
CLERK: "Certainly. What size?"
CHILD: "I don't know, but I wear a size five hat!"

What goes "Ha, ha, ha, plop!"?

Someone laughing his head off.

What must one do to have soft hands?

Nothing.

POLICE OFFICER (to boy sitting in an oak tree): "What are you doing way up there?"

BOY: "I don't know. I must have sat on an acorn!"

What is larger when cut at both ends?

A ditch.

TEACHER: "Sally, what would you do if a man-eating tiger were chasing you?"

SALLY: "Nothing — I'm a *girl*!"

Why does that letter bring tears to your eyes?

It's written on onion skin.

What is it that looks like a cat, eats like a cat, walks like a cat, and yet is not a cat?

A kitten.

Which is the largest room in the world?

Room for improvement.

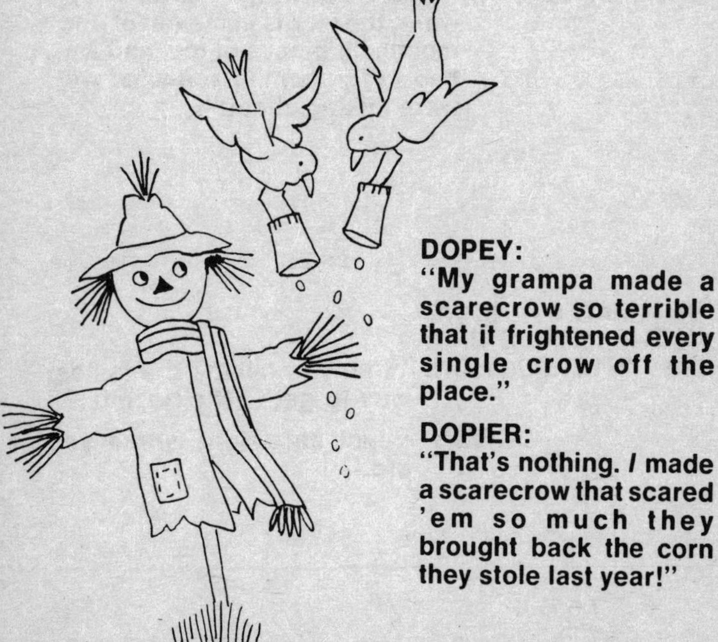

DOPEY:
"My grampa made a scarecrow so terrible that it frightened every single crow off the place."

DOPIER:
"That's nothing. *I* made a scarecrow that scared 'em so much they brought back the corn they stole last year!"

ARCTIC EXPLORER: "It was so cold where we were, that the candle froze and we couldn't blow it out."

RIVAL EXPLORER: "That's nothing — where *we* were, the words came out of our mouths in pieces of ice, and we had to *fry* them to see what we were talking about!"

YOUNG MAN STANDING IN THE MIDDLE OF A BUSY INTERSECTION: "Can you tell me the fastest way to get to the hospital?"

DRIVER: "Just stay right where you are."

What is the beginning of eternity, the end of time and space, the beginning of every end and the end of every place?

The letter E.

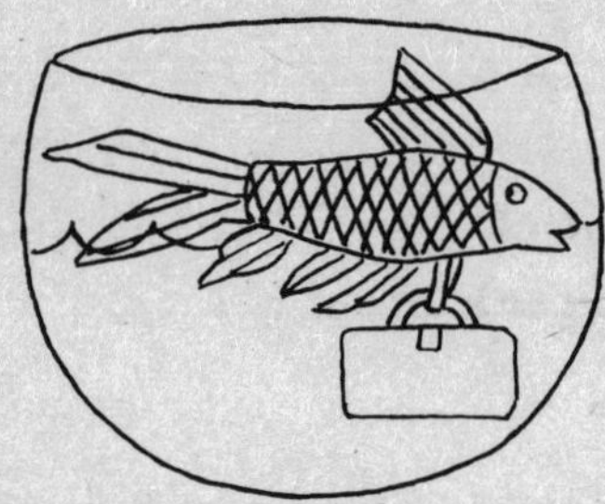

TEACHER:
"Peter, can you tell me the name of an animal that travels great distances?"

PETER:
"A goldfish. It travels around the globe."

What is taken from you before you get it?

Your portrait.

BIG BROTHER: "Well, Joey, how do you like school?"

JOEY: "Closed."

What has spots, 16 wheels, and a long neck?

A giraffe on roller skates.

What kind of coat is made without sleeves and put on wet?

A coat of paint.

Why does the moon go to the bank?

To change quarters.

Why is a goose like an icicle?

Because they both grow down.

A man dropped in to pay his friend a visit, and was amazed to find the friend playing chess with his dog. The man watched in silence for a few minutes, then burst out with, "That's the smartest dog I ever saw in my life!"

"Oh, he isn't so smart," was the owner's answer. "I've beaten him three games out of four today!"

What dog keeps the best time?

A watchdog.

What toe never grows a corn?

Mistletoe.

What do you call a carpenter who lends his tools to his neighbor?

A saw loser.

TEACHER: "Name three collective nouns."

BILLY: "Fly-paper, waste-basket, and vacuum-cleaner."

MARK: I have a dog that has no tail.
MARY: Then how can you tell when he's happy?
MARK: He stops biting.

Can February March?

No, but April May.

Why do lions eat raw meat?

They can't cook.

How did the musician clean his dirty tuba?

With a tuba toothpaste.

Why did the weatherman lose his job?

The weather didn't agree with him.

Why is the sea restless?

Because it has rocks in its bed.

What's the best way to prevent infection caused by biting insects?

Don't bite any.